Dedicated to all our former coaches and fellow weekend warriors. Remember, they're only games, so, lighten up and have a laugh.

Especially for:

____

ISBN: 1-56245-021-2 Printed in the U.S.A.

"Being with a woman all night never hurt no professional baseball player. It's the staying up all night looking for one that does him in."

Casey Stengel
Former Major League Manager

Men have three secret wishes — to outsmart race-horses, women and fish.

"My wife made me a millionaire. I used to have three million."

Bobby Hull
Hall of Fame Hockey Player, on his divorce.

"It took me seventeen years to get three thousand hits in baseball. I did it in one afternoon on the golf course."

Hank Aaron
All Time Home-Run King

"I don't jog. If I die, I want to be sick."

Abe Lemons
College Basketball Coach

"My knees look like they lost a knife fight with a midget."

E. J. Holub

Former Kansas City Chiefs Linebacker, on his 12 knee operations.

"I seldom serve aces. Most of mine are jokers."

"Everybody says they'll marry till death, and they're divorced a few weeks later. I've lied to the judge twice myself."

Muhammad Ali
Former Heavyweight Boxing Champion

"He's a perfectionist. If he was married to Racquel Welch, he'd expect her to cook."

Don Meredith

Former Cowboy quarterback, on coach Tom Landry.

"Putting a fighter in the business world is like putting silk stockings on a pig."

Jack Hurley
Boxing Manager

"Work: a dangerous disorder affecting high public functionaries who want to go fishing."

Ambrose Bierce

"Well, I won't say I can or I can't: But if I do, I do it before most people get up in the morning."

Bear Bryant
College football coach on whether it's true he can walk on water.

"My doctor recently told me that jogging could add years to my life. I think he was right. I feel ten years older already."

Milton Berle

"Tennis is a perfect combination of violent action taking place in an atmosphere of tranquility."

Billy Jean King

"When I was a little boy, I wanted to be a baseball player, and join the circus. With the Yankees, I've accomplished both."

Craig Nettles
Former New York Yankees Third Baseman

"I left because of illness and fatigue. The fans were sick and tired of me."

John Ralston
Former Coach of the Denver Broncos

"If I ever need a brain transplant, I want one from a sportswriter, because I'll know it's never been used."

Joe Paterno
Penn State Football Coach

"I never graduated from Iowa. I was only there for two terms — Truman's and Eisenhower's."

Alex Karras
Former NFL Defensive Lineman

"Fishing: a sport played with a long pole that has a worm at one end and a fool at the other."

"I took a little English, a little math, some science, a few hubcaps and some wheelcovers."

Gates Brown
Major league outfielder, recalling high school.

"I learned a long time ago that minor surgery is when they do the operation on someone else, not you."

Bill Walton
Former San Diego Clippers Center

"Hit at the girl whenever possible."

Bill Tilden
on how to play effective mixed doubles.

"I have a friend who is a nun, and her social life is better than mine."

Wendy Turnbull

Tennis player, on her social life during the playing season.

"For most amateurs, the best wood in the bag is the pencil."

Chi Chi Rodriguez
Professional Golfer

"Drop shots are my specialty; I hit a shot and drop another point."

"I wouldn't ever set out to hurt anybody deliberately unless it was, you know, important — like a league game or something."

Dick Butkus
Chicago Bear Hall of Famer

"I have a lifetime contract. That means I can't be fired during the third quarter if we're ahead and moving the ball."

Lou Holtz
Notre Dame University Football Coach.

"Trying to sneak a pitch past Hank Aaron is like trying to sneak the sunrise past a rooster."

Joe Adcock
Former Major League Baseball player

"The only difference between me and General Custer is that I have to watch the films on Sunday."

Rick Venturi
College Football Coach

"Son, looks to me like you're spending too much time on one subject."

Shelby Metcalf
College basketball coach, to a player who received four F's and and a D.

"Absolute silence — That's the one thing a sports-writer can quote accurately.

Bobby Knight
Indiana Basketball Coach

"All the fat guys watch me and say to their wives, "See, there's a fat guy doing okay. Bring me another beer."

Mickey Lolich
Former Detroit Tigers Pitcher

"Last season we couldn't win at home and we were losing on the road. My failure as a coach was that I couldn't think of anyplace else to play."

Harry Neale
Professional Hockey Coach

"Blind people come to the park just to listen to him pitch."

Reggie Jackson
Commenting on Tom Seaver.

"I just wrap my arms around the whole backfield and peel 'em off one by one until I get to the ball carrier. Him I keep."

Big Daddy Lipscomb
Former NFL defensive tackle, on his tackling technique.

"I went to a fight the other night, and a hockey game broke out."

Rodney Dangerfield

How far a fisherman stretches the truth depends on the length of his arms.

To be a success at fishing you should get there yesterday, when the fish were biting.

"I like the people, the talk, even the dinners. I love everything about hockey except the game.

Glenn Hall
NHL Goaltender

Fishing is a sport that makes men and truth strangers.

"Who ever said, 'It's not whether you win or lose that counts,' probably lost."

Martina Navratilova

"The film looks suspiciously like the game itself."

Bum Phillips

Former NFL coach, after viewing a lopsided loss to the Atlanta Falcons.

"Just once I'd like to see the win-loss records of doctors right out front where people could see them — won ten, lost three, tied two."

Abe Lemons
Former Texas basketball coach

"You've just one problem. You stand too close to the ball — after you've hit it."

Sam Snead
Advice to a pupil.

"When you win, you eat better, sleep better and your beer tastes better. And your wife looks like Gina Lollobrigida."

Johnny Pesky
Boston Red Sox Manager

"I don't mind starting a season with unknowns. I just don't like finishing a season with a bunch of them."

Lou Holtz
Football Coach
Notre Dame University

Nothing grows faster than a fish from the time he bites until the time he gets away.

"Remember, Coach, we're all behind you — win or tie."

Anonymous Alumnus
Writing in a telegram to the football coach before a big game.

"I hate to lose more than I like to win."

Jimmy Conners

"Taylor, we've run out of time outs. Go in there and get hurt."

George Halas
Former Chicago Bears Coach

"When you're playing for the national championship, it's not a matter of life or death. It's more important than that."

Duffy Daugherty
Former Michigan State Football Coach

"There are two types of coaches. Them that have just been fired, and them that are going to be fired."

Bum Phillips
Former NFL Coach

"Losers have tons of variety. Champions take pride in just learning to hit the same old boring winners."

Vic Braden

"It's good sportsmanship to not pick up lost golf balls while they are still rolling."

Mark Twain

"I'm working as hard as I can to get my life and my cash to run out at the same time. If I can just die after lunch Tuesday, every-thing will be perfect."

Doug Sanders
Former Professional Golfer

"My uncle always described an unforced error as his first marriage."

Bud Collins
Former Tennis Pro

"With the money I'm making, I should be playing two positions."

Pete Rose
Retired Coach and Baseball Player

"People always ask me if success is going to change me, and I tell them I sure hope so."

Randy "Tex" Cobb
Heavyweight boxer

"I won't know until my barber tells me on Monday."

Knute Rockne
When asked after a game why Notre Dame had lost.

"When they operated, I told them to put in a Koufax fastball. They did — but it was Mrs. Koufax's."

Tommy John

Former N.Y. Yankees Pitcher recalling his 1974 arm surgery.

"Because if it didn't work out, I didn't want to blow the whole day."

Paul Horning

Former Green Bay Packers running back, on why his marriage ceremony was before noon.

"We were tipping off our plays. Whenever we broke from the huddle, three backs were laughing and one was as pale as a ghost."

John Breen

"Statistics always remind me of the fellow who drowned in a river whose average depth was only three feet."

Woody Hayes
Ohio State Football Coach

"Hey, is this room out of bounds?"

Alex Karras

Former NFL defensive lineman, to a startled employee, after hitting a golf ball off the first tee through a large plate glass window in the clubhouse.

"When I'm on the road, my greatest ambition is to get a standing boo."

Al Hrabosky
Former Major League Relief Pitcher

Tennis:

The only game where love means nothing.

"I'd get real close to him and breathe on his goggles.

Johnny Kerr

Sportscaster and former NBA player and coach, on how he would guard Kareem Abdul-Jabbar.

"The country is full of good coaches. What it takes to win is a bunch of interested players."

Don Coryell
Former San Diego Chargers Coach

"When it's third and ten, you can take the milk drinkers and I'll take the whiskey drinkers every time."

Max McGee
Former Green Bay Packers Receiver

"Our biggest concern this season will be diaper rash."

George MacIntyre
College football coach, surveying a roster that included 26 freshmen and 25 sophomores.

"Who's the one guy who thinks we can do it?"

Mike Gottfried
Kansas Football Coach, on learning that the odds against his Jayhawks winning the Big Eight title are 100 to 1.

"If I only had a little humility I would be perfect."

Ted Turner
Atlanta Braves and Hawks Owner

"I don't know. I only played there nine years."

Walt Garrison

Former Dallas Cowboys Fullback, when asked if coach Tom Landry ever smiles.

"Fishing, with me, has always been an excuse to drink in the daytime."

Jimmy Cannon

The typical fisherman is long on optimism and short on memory.

"There are still over sixty million Chinese who don't care if we win or lose."

John McKay
Former College and Professional Football Coach

"I had a better year than he did."

Babe Ruth

Hall of Fame outfielder, when told that President Hoover made less than the $80,000 Ruth was demanding in 1930.

Other Great Quotations Books:

- Happy Birthday
- Aged to Perfection
- Retirement
- Love on Your Wedding Day
- Thank You
- Thinking of You
- Words of Love
- Words for Friendship
- Inspirations
- Sports Poop
- Over the Hill
- Golf Humor
- Happy Birthday to the Golfer
- Handle Stress
- A Smiles Increases Your Face Value
- Keys to Happiness
- Things You'll Learn...
- Teachers Inspirations
- Boyfriends Live Longer than ...
- The Complete Bathroom Reader
- Our Life Together
- Thoughts from the Heart
- An Apple a Day
- The Joy of Family
- What to Tell Your Children
- The Book of Proverbs
- A Friend is a Present

GREAT QUOTATIONS, INC.
919 SPRINGER DRIVE • LOMBARD, IL 60148-6416

TOLL FREE: 800-621-1432 (outside Illinois)
(708) 953-1222